CARL PIE

A Legacy of Innovation and
Ethics in Technology.

Jason M. Oliver

TABLE OF CONTENTS

INTRODUCTION

The rapid growth of technology has fundamentally changed how societies operate. As we stand at the precipice of a new age of digital innovation, the role of influential figures in shaping these advancements cannot be understated. One such figure is Carl Pi, a tech entrepreneur whose vision and values have significantly impacted the technological landscape, particularly in the realm of data analytics, surveillance and the ethical considerations surrounding these domains.

Technology, with its ability to shape economies, politics, and daily lives, offers vast opportunities for progress. But it also presents unique challenges that demand careful consideration. As powerful technologies like artificial intelligence (AI), big data and machine learning evolve, they introduce dilemmas about privacy, governance and the balance between public good and individual rights. At the center of this conversation is Carl Pi, who stands as a visionary and a controversial figure in how technology is used, governed and understood. This book will explore Carl Pi's legacy, focusing not only on his technological innovations but also on the ethical and moral questions that arise from those innovations. As we delve into his life and career, we will uncover the multifaceted aspects of his influence, from the technical marvels he helped create to the important questions his work raises about privacy, security, and democracy.

The relationship between technology and ethics is not a simple one, and Pi's journey provides a lens through which to examine the tensions that exist between progress and accountability. As we explore these themes, we will ask whether it's possible to push the boundaries of innovation while safeguarding ethical principles and public trust.

In the book, we will trace Carl Pi's rise from humble beginnings to the global stage, where his ideas and innovations have made a lasting impact. We will discuss how his contributions to the tech world, particularly through companies like Palantir, have transformed industries, and how these innovations raise important questions about surveillance, data use and government influence. we will explore the ethical implications of these technologies. What does it mean for privacy when vast amounts of personal data are collected and analyzed? How do we ensure transparency and accountability when powerful companies and governments use these technologies to monitor and influence society? These are just some of the critical questions that Carl Pi's work brings to the forefront.

This book is not just an exploration of Pi's achievements, but also a reflection on the broader implications of technology in our world. It will challenge readers to think deeply about the role of innovation in shaping our future and how we can create a technology-driven society that prioritizes ethical principles and democratic values.

By examining Carl Pi's story, this book aims to spark conversation about how we approach the complex relationship between technology and ethics, and how we can build a future where innovation serves the greater good. Through his legacy, we will better understand the promises and perils of a world increasingly driven by technology, and the responsibility we all share in shaping that world for the generations to come.

CHAPTER 1: THE RISE OF CARL PI IN THE TECH WORLD

Carl Pi's journey from a young, aspiring entrepreneur to a major figure in the tech world is one that mirrors the growth and transformation of the digital landscape itself. From the early days of the internet to the modern age of artificial intelligence (AI), data analytics, and surveillance technologies, Pi has been at the forefront of many groundbreaking innovations. His story is one of ambition, vision, and an unwavering commitment to shaping the future of technology, but it also raises important questions about the ethical responsibilities of those who create and wield such technologies.

Technology's Growing Impact on Society

To understand Carl Pi's rise in the tech world, it's essential to first examine the broader context in which he emerged. Over the past few decades, technology has evolved at an unprecedented rate, reshaping industries, economies and societies. The digital revolution, driven by the rise of the internet, smartphones and cloud computing, has brought about profound changes in the way we communicate, work and live.

But as technology has advanced, so too has its influence on society. Digital platforms have transformed communication, social interactions, and even political discourse. The internet has become a tool for education, entertainment, commerce and activism. At the same time, these advancements have introduced new challenges, particularly around issues of privacy, security and data ownership. With the vast amounts of personal data generated by online activities, questions about how this data is used and who controls it have become central to discussions about technology's role in society.

In this environment, Carl Pi emerged as a figure who sought to harness the power of technology to address complex problems. As the founder of Palantir, Pi focused on building software that could analyze and interpret vast amounts of data to solve critical challenges in areas like national security, healthcare and finance. His company's software has been used by governments and corporations around the world, enabling them to make data-driven decisions with unprecedented precision. However, this success has not been without controversy, particularly around the ethical implications of how this data is collected, used, and shared.

Pi's work exemplifies the growing impact of technology on society and highlights the need for a balanced approach to innovation one that not only seeks to maximize benefits but also takes into account the ethical ramifications of those innovations. As technology continues to evolve, Pi's legacy will serve as a case study for how we can navigate the opportunities and challenges presented by digital advancements.

Setting the Stage: Ethics and Innovation

One of the defining characteristics of Carl Pi's career has been his ability to blend innovation with a deep concern for the ethical implications of his work. Pi has consistently sought to create technologies that can solve real-world problems, but he has also been at the forefront of discussions about the ethical responsibility of tech companies, especially those dealing with sensitive data.

From the very beginning of Palantir, Pi understood the potential risks and rewards associated with data analytics. His vision was not just about building powerful tools but also about ensuring that these tools were used responsibly. Palantir's software, which allows users to analyze vast amounts of data to uncover patterns and insights, has been used in a variety of industries, from government and law enforcement to healthcare and finance. However, its use in surveillance and intelligence gathering has raised concerns about privacy, civil liberties, and the potential for abuse.

Pi's commitment to ethical innovation can be seen in his approach to the company's partnerships and projects. For example, Palantir has been involved in projects with government agencies, such as the U.S. Department of Defense and the Central Intelligence Agency (CIA). While these partnerships have been instrumental in helping the government address security threats, they have also led to criticism, particularly from privacy advocates who argue that the company's technology could be used to infringe on individual freedoms. Despite the controversies surrounding his work, Pi has consistently defended his company's mission, arguing that the benefits of data-driven decision-making outweigh the risks. He has also emphasized the importance of transparency and accountability in the use of technology. In this regard, Pi has positioned himself as a leader in the ongoing conversation about how to balance innovation with ethical considerations.

As we explore Carl Pi's rise in the tech world, it becomes clear that his success is not just a result of his technical expertise or business acumen, but also his ability to navigate the ethical complexities of the digital age. The challenges he has faced in balancing the demands of innovation with the need for responsible use of technology are not unique to him but reflect broader tensions in the tech industry today.

Carl Pi's Vision for the Future of Technology

At the heart of Carl Pi's rise in the tech world is his visionary approach to the future of technology. While many in the tech industry focus on the immediate applications of their products and services, Pi has always looked beyond the present, considering how technology will evolve and what impact it will have on society.

Pi's vision for the future of technology is centered on the idea that data is the key to solving some of the world's most pressing challenges. Whether it's improving healthcare outcomes, addressing climate change, or enhancing national security, Pi believes that data analytics can provide the insights needed to make informed, effective decisions. He also recognizes that the power of data comes with great responsibility.

One of Pi's central goals has been to ensure that technology serves the greater good, rather than simply advancing the interests of corporations or governments. He has long argued that technology should be used to empower individuals, improve societies, and create a more equitable world. This vision has been a driving force behind his work at Palantir, where he has sought to develop tools that can help organizations make better decisions while also upholding ethical standards. As Pi looks to the future, he remains committed to developing technologies that address the complexities of the modern world. However, he also recognizes that the rapid pace of technological change presents significant challenges, particularly when it comes to issues of privacy, security, and governance. These challenges will require not only innovative solutions but also careful consideration of the ethical implications of new technologies. Carl Pi's rise in the tech world is a testament to the power of visionary thinking and the potential of technology to change the world. But it is also a reminder that with great power comes great responsibility. As Pi continues to shape the future of technology, his legacy will be defined not only by the innovations he has introduced but also by how he has navigated the ethical complexities of a rapidly changing digital landscape.

CHAPTER 2: CARL PI'S EARLY YEARS AND VISIONARY ROOTS

Carl Pi's journey from a young, ambitious individual to one of the most influential figures in the world of technology is rooted in his early experiences, values and the formative influences that shaped his worldview. Before becoming a tech mogul and the face of Palantir, Pi's childhood and adolescence laid the foundation for the innovation, risk-taking, and ethical considerations that would define his career. This chapter explores his early years, the inspirations behind his innovations, and the pivotal moments that shaped his path toward building one of the most significant companies in the tech industry.

From Humble Beginnings to Tech Mogul

Carl Pi was born into a family where technology and innovation were not the immediate focal points. Raised in a middle-class environment, he didn't come from a background of vast wealth or privilege. Yet, from a young age, he showed an extraordinary aptitude for understanding complex systems and a fascination with how things worked. Pi's interest in technology began with an early curiosity about computers, which at the time were still relatively new and inaccessible to many people.

He spent much of his early years tinkering with computers, learning programming languages, and experimenting with software development. This self-driven approach to learning was a precursor to the entrepreneurial mindset that would later define his career. Unlike many of his peers, who followed traditional academic routes, Pi sought out opportunities to learn on his own. He was not content with just understanding how things worked; he was deeply interested in why they worked the way they did and how they could be improved.

Pi's early experiences with technology were marked by a sense of independence and a desire to break free from conventional structures. Instead of relying solely on formal education, he immersed himself in hands-on experiences, participating in projects that allowed him to develop both technical skills and a unique perspective on problem-solving. This approach to learning would later translate into his work at Palantir, where the focus was on innovation, data-driven solutions, and creating systems that could address real-world challenges.

Pi's journey wasn't solely about personal growth and technical skills. His background in a modest household instilled in him a strong work ethic and an understanding of the value of perseverance. He wasn't born into a legacy of wealth or influence, but rather built his career from the ground up, proving that with determination and vision, one could challenge the status quo and make a significant impact in the world of technology.

The Inspiration Behind Carl Pi's Innovations

Carl Pi's vision for the future of technology was not solely shaped by his own experiences but also by the broader technological and social environment of the time. Growing up in an era where the internet was becoming a transformative force, Pi witnessed firsthand the vast potential of digital technologies to revolutionize various industries. The rapid rise of the internet, coupled with the proliferation of personal computers, laid the groundwork for his belief that data could be the key to solving complex global challenges.

One of the major inspirations behind Pi's innovations was the belief that technology should not just serve the interests of the wealthy or powerful but should be used to address societal problems. He was particularly drawn to the potential of data analytics to improve decision-making in critical areas such as national security, healthcare, and law enforcement.

Unlike other entrepreneurs who focused primarily on consumer-facing technologies, Pi recognized that data had the power to unlock new insights that could have profound social implications.

His interest in data-driven solutions was further reinforced during his time at university, where he studied computer science and engineering. At university, Pi encountered professors and mentors who challenged him to think beyond traditional approaches to problem-solving. They encouraged him to explore how technology could be leveraged for the greater good and to consider the ethical implications of the technologies he was developing. This early exposure to the ethical dimensions of technology would have a lasting impact on Pi's approach to innovation.

Pi was also inspired by the success stories of other tech visionaries who had come before him. Figures like Steve Jobs and Bill Gates, who transformed industries through innovation, were role models for Pi. However, unlike these figures, Pi sought to combine business success with a focus on societal good. He believed that technology could be a force for positive change, but it was essential to approach it with a sense of responsibility and caution.

Pi's unique combination of technical expertise, business acumen, and ethical considerations became the foundation for his innovations. He was driven by the idea that technology could make a real difference in the world, but only if it was developed and used in ways that prioritized both efficacy and responsibility.

Early Influences and Pivotal Moments

Carl Pi's path to founding Palantir was shaped by several key influences and pivotal moments in his life. Early exposure to the tech industry, combined with formative experiences in his personal and academic life, set him on a course that would lead to the creation of one of the most important companies in the world of data analytics and surveillance.

One of the most pivotal moments in Pi's early life was his exposure to the complexities of government and intelligence work. During his time at university, Pi became interested in the intersection of technology and national security, particularly in how data could be used to prevent threats and improve intelligence operations. This interest led him to develop relationships with key figures in the government and military, providing him with the opportunity to explore how technology could be applied to solve some of the most pressing issues facing the nation. At the same time, Pi's exposure to the business world and his early work experiences provided him with the entrepreneurial drive to take risks and push boundaries. He worked at several tech companies before founding Palantir, learning the ins and outs of the industry and building connections with like-minded individuals who shared his passion for innovation. These experiences were critical in shaping Pi's understanding of the tech landscape and refining his vision for the future.

Another pivotal moment came when Pi began to realize the vast potential of data analytics. He saw how organizations were increasingly relying on data to make decisions but also noticed the limitations of traditional methods of analyzing data. The idea for Palantir began to take shape as Pi recognized that there was a need for a more sophisticated approach to data analysis one that could uncover hidden patterns and offer insights that could drive meaningful action. This realization would lead to the creation of Palantir, a company designed to address the complexities of data analysis in sectors such as government, healthcare, and finance.

Pi's ability to see patterns where others saw challenges, and his belief that technology could be used to solve global problems, were central to his early success. His work was not simply about creating software; it was about changing how people viewed data and its potential impact on society.

CHAPTER 3: SHAPING THE

MODERN TECH LANDSCAPE

Carl Pi's innovations have not only shaped the trajectory of Palantir, but they have also made a significant mark on the broader tech landscape. His vision of data analytics as a tool to drive decision-making has influenced industries ranging from government and national security to healthcare and finance. Pi's work, however, is not just about creating cutting-edge technology; it's also about pushing the boundaries of what technology can do in the service of solving complex global problems. This chapter explores how Pi's groundbreaking work has shaped the modern tech landscape, the role of artificial intelligence (AI) and machine learning in his vision, and how his innovations have bridged the gap between technological advancement and ethical responsibility.

Pioneering Solutions in Data and Surveillance

The core of Carl Pi's legacy lies in his pioneering work in data analytics and surveillance technologies. At the heart of Palantir's mission is the development of software that enables organizations to analyze vast amounts of data to uncover insights that might otherwise remain hidden. Pi's vision was clear: by leveraging big data, powerful algorithms, and sophisticated analytics, it would be possible to tackle some of the world's most pressing challenges.

Data analytics, when properly harnessed, can provide invaluable insights into areas such as crime prevention, terrorism prevention, public health and disaster response. Pi saw the potential for data to not just aid decision-making but also to provide actionable intelligence that could lead to concrete, positive outcomes. Palantir's software became a critical tool for government agencies and organizations working in fields that require fast, accurate, and data-driven decisions, such as intelligence and law enforcement.

Pi's innovations also sparked controversy, particularly in the realm of surveillance. The ability to gather, analyze, and interpret vast amounts of data whether from individuals, governments, or private entities has raised significant concerns about privacy, civil liberties, and the potential for abuse. Critics argue that the technology could be used to infringe upon personal freedoms, while supporters contend that it's a necessary tool for safeguarding national security and addressing urgent social issues.

Despite these concerns, Pi has defended the role of surveillance technologies, emphasizing their potential to protect citizens and prevent harm. He has argued that when used responsibly and transparently, surveillance technologies can be a force for good. However, the ethical questions surrounding data collection, particularly in the areas of privacy and consent, remain a crucial challenge that Pi and others in the tech world must navigate as these technologies continue to evolve.

The Role of AI and Machine Learning in Carl Pi's Vision

Artificial intelligence (AI) and machine learning (ML) are at the heart of Carl Pi's vision for the future of technology. These technologies have the potential to revolutionize industries and transform the way we live and work. Pi was one of the early pioneers in recognizing the transformative power of AI and ML in solving complex problems, particularly in the context of big data analytics.

At Palantir, AI and ML are integral components of the software tools that help organizations process and interpret massive datasets. These technologies allow for automated pattern recognition, predictive modeling, and real-time decision-making, which can provide valuable insights in sectors ranging from government intelligence to healthcare and financial services. For example, AI and ML algorithms are used to predict criminal activity, track potential threats, and identify emerging patterns in data that might otherwise go unnoticed.

But Pi's use of AI and ML has always been grounded in the belief that these technologies should be used responsibly. As powerful as these tools are, they also raise important ethical questions about bias, fairness, and accountability. Pi has been vocal about the need for transparency in AI and ML algorithms, recognizing that without proper oversight, these technologies could perpetuate existing biases or lead to unintended consequences.

In many ways, Pi's approach to AI and ML reflects his broader philosophy of ethical innovation. He understands that while these technologies can drive significant progress, they must be developed and implemented with caution and care. As AI and ML continue to evolve, Pi remains committed to ensuring that they are used to improve lives, not to exploit vulnerabilities or create new ethical dilemmas.

Bridging the Gap Between Innovation and Ethics

Carl Pi's impact on the tech world goes beyond his technical expertise.

He has also been a key figure in bridging the gap between technological innovation and ethical responsibility. As technology becomes more powerful, the potential for its misuse grows exponentially. Pi has consistently emphasized that with great innovation comes the need for great responsibility, particularly when it comes to how data is used, shared, and protected.

One of the most significant ways Pi has sought to bridge this gap is through his commitment to transparency and accountability. At Palantir, Pi has worked to ensure that the company's software is used in ways that respect privacy and human rights. This includes implementing safeguards to prevent the misuse of data and providing customers with the tools they need to make ethical decisions when using Palantir's technology.

Pi has also been an advocate for the development of ethical standards in the tech industry. As data-driven technologies continue to evolve, Pi has argued that tech companies must take the lead in creating frameworks for responsible innovation. This includes addressing issues like data privacy, algorithmic bias, and the ethical implications of surveillance. By encouraging dialogue and collaboration between technologists, policymakers, and ethicists, Pi hopes to create a future where technology serves the greater good and operates within a framework of shared values. While Pi's commitment to ethics is clear, it is not always easy to reconcile with the demands of business and innovation. The tension between profit and responsibility is a constant challenge, and Pi has faced criticism for some of the ethical dilemmas associated with Palantir's work. However, he has remained steadfast in his belief that technology can be a force for positive change if developed and used with the right intentions and safeguards.

As Pi continues to shape the future of technology, his efforts to bridge the gap between innovation and ethics will play a critical role in determining how technology evolves and the role it will play in society. The work of Pi and others in the tech industry will set the standard for how we navigate the complex relationship between technological progress and ethical responsibility.

CHAPTER 4: ETHICS AND RESPONSIBILITY IN A DATA-DRIVEN WORLD

As technology continues to evolve at an exponential rate, the ethical implications of these advancements have become a central focus of debate. Carl Pi, as a pioneer in the field of data analytics and surveillance, has often found himself at the center of these discussions. At the core of Pi's work is a deep recognition that data is not just a tool for progress but also carries significant ethical responsibility. This chapter explores the delicate balance between innovation and ethical considerations, looking at the challenges of protecting privacy, the moral implications of surveillance technologies, and Pi's approach to ensuring transparency and accountability in a world increasingly driven by data.

Balancing Profit and Privacy

The rapid growth of data analytics, particularly in industries such as finance, healthcare, and national security, has brought about a fundamental shift in how businesses and governments operate. Data has become a powerful commodity, and companies like Palantir have capitalized on the ability to collect, analyze, and interpret vast amounts of personal and organizational information. However, this ability to process and utilize data also comes with significant ethical challenges, particularly when it comes to privacy. One of the most pressing ethical dilemmas in Pi's work is how to balance the potential profits of data-driven solutions with the protection of individual privacy. While data analytics offers immense value to businesses and governments, it also raises questions about how much personal information should be collected, who controls that data, and how it should be used. Pi's Palantir platform is a prime example of this tension: the software is capable of analyzing vast amounts of data, uncovering patterns and providing insights that can drive important decisions in fields such as public health and national security. However, the very same capabilities that allow for these insights also open the door to surveillance and the potential violation of privacy.

Pi has faced criticism for Palantir's role in data collection and surveillance, particularly given the sensitive nature of the information that the company's software can access. Critics argue that the widespread collection of personal data—often without explicit consent from individuals undermines privacy rights and can be used for exploitative purposes. For example, Palantir's involvement in government surveillance programs, such as those operated by the U.S. Department of Defense and law enforcement agencies, has raised concerns about the overreach of surveillance and the potential for abuse of power.

Pi has consistently defended his company's role, arguing that the benefits of using data to solve pressing societal problems far outweigh the potential risks. He believes that when used responsibly, data can be a force for good, helping to protect public safety, combat terrorism, and improve healthcare outcomes. However, he also acknowledges that there is a fine line between using data for the common good and exploiting it for profit or power. Pi has advocated for a framework of ethical guidelines to govern how data is collected, analyzed, and used, emphasizing that privacy protections must be built into the foundation of any data-driven system.

Balancing profit and privacy is a complex challenge, and Pi's work is an example of the struggle to navigate this delicate equilibrium. His approach to this issue has been one of transparency and careful consideration of the ethical consequences of each decision. As data continues to grow as a valuable resource, the question of how to balance these competing interests will remain a critical consideration for Pi and other leaders in the tech industry.

The Moral Implications of Surveillance Technology

The use of surveillance technology, particularly in the form of data analytics and monitoring systems, has become one of the most contentious issues in the modern tech landscape. Pi's Palantir has been at the center of debates about the ethical implications of surveillance. The company's software is capable of collecting and analyzing data from a variety of sources social media, government databases, and private organizations to track patterns and identify potential threats. While these capabilities have been lauded for their ability to prevent crime, terrorism, and other societal risks, they also raise serious moral questions about the balance between security and individual freedoms.

The primary moral concern surrounding surveillance technology is its potential to infringe on civil liberties. Critics argue that the widespread use of surveillance tools can lead to an erosion of privacy, particularly when individuals are unaware that their data is being collected and analyzed. The rise of mass surveillance, fueled by powerful data analytics platforms like Palantir, has led to fears of a "Big Brother" society, where governments and corporations have unprecedented access to personal information.

Pi has faced scrutiny over Palantir's involvement in surveillance, especially in cases where the company's software has been used to track individuals without their consent. For example, Palantir's collaboration with government agencies in the U.S. has led to concerns about the surveillance of ordinary citizens and the potential for abuse. Despite this criticism, Pi has defended the ethical value of Palantir's work, asserting that the technology is used to protect citizens from harm, not to infringe on their rights.

At the heart of the moral debate surrounding surveillance is the issue of consent. Many individuals are unaware of the extent to which their personal information is being collected and analyzed, which raises questions about whether they should have a say in how their data is used. Pi has acknowledged this concern and has called for greater transparency in how data is collected and used. He has argued that individuals should have more control over their own data, but he also believes that there are situations where the need for security and the protection of society must outweigh individual privacy concerns.

Pi's work highlights the complex moral landscape that technology companies must navigate when developing surveillance systems. While the potential benefits of such systems are undeniable, the ethical implications must be carefully considered to ensure that they are used in ways that respect fundamental human rights.

Carl Pi's Stance on Transparency and Accountability

One of the defining aspects of Carl Pi's approach to technology is his unwavering commitment to transparency and accountability. While he has faced criticism for the ethical implications of Palantir's work, he has consistently advocated for greater transparency in how data is used and how decisions are made. This commitment to openness is grounded in his belief that technology should serve society's best interests, and that the risks associated with powerful tools must be mitigated through clear oversight.

Transparency is particularly important in the realm of data analytics and surveillance, where the stakes are high and the potential for misuse is significant. Pi has called for more robust regulatory frameworks to ensure that technology companies operate within clear ethical guidelines. He has argued that the tech industry must take responsibility for the impact of its innovations, particularly when they affect individuals' privacy and security.

In addition to advocating for transparency in data usage, Pi has also emphasized the need for accountability in the development and deployment of surveillance technologies. He has argued that technology companies must be held accountable for the ethical implications of their products, and that those who create powerful tools must be prepared to answer for their impact on society. This includes ensuring that technology is not used to manipulate or control individuals, but rather to serve the public good.

Pi's stance on transparency and accountability reflects his broader commitment to ethical innovation. While he recognizes that data analytics and surveillance technologies have the potential to transform industries and solve complex problems, he remains steadfast in his belief that these technologies must be developed and used with integrity. By championing transparency and accountability, Pi has set an example for other leaders in the tech industry, urging them to consider the long-term consequences of their innovations and to prioritize ethical considerations alongside technical advancements.

CHAPTER 5: THE INTERSECTION OF INNOVATION AND GOVERNANCE

As technology becomes increasingly integrated into every facet of society, the role of governance in regulating and shaping the future of innovation has never been more crucial. Carl Pi has consistently been at the forefront of discussions about how governments and tech companies should interact to ensure that technological advancements benefit society while minimizing harm. This chapter delves into the complex relationship between innovation and governance, exploring regulatory challenges in the tech industry, Pi's advocacy for ethical standards, and his contributions to policy and governance that aim to create a more responsible framework for technological development.

Regulatory Challenges in Tech Innovation

The rapid pace of technological development poses significant challenges for regulators and policymakers around the world. As companies like Palantir push the boundaries of data analytics, artificial intelligence (AI), and surveillance technologies, the need for effective regulation has become increasingly apparent. The problem, however, lies in the ability of governments to keep up with the speed of innovation. Laws and regulations that were designed for a slower-moving technological landscape often struggle to address the complexities of the modern digital age.

One of the core challenges in regulating tech innovation is ensuring that new technologies do not outpace the ability of lawmakers and regulators to understand and govern them effectively. Many of the technologies that Pi and Palantir work with such as AI, machine learning, and big data analytics are evolving at such a rapid rate that traditional forms of governance often fail to address their unique characteristics. For example, Palantir's data analytics software can analyze vast amounts of information in real time, uncovering insights that might otherwise take years to discover. This creates a dilemma for regulators, who must balance the need for innovation with the responsibility to protect privacy, ensure fairness, and prevent misuse.

The global nature of the tech industry presents its own set of regulatory challenges. Many tech companies operate across borders, which complicates efforts to establish consistent regulatory frameworks. Different countries have different approaches to data protection, privacy rights, and surveillance, creating a patchwork of regulations that can be difficult for both companies and governments to navigate. Pi has been vocal about the need for international collaboration and the development of global standards that can guide the responsible use of emerging technologies.

As the demand for new technologies continues to grow, Pi has argued that it is essential for governments to engage with the tech industry and work together to develop appropriate regulatory frameworks. Rather than adopting an adversarial stance, Pi believes that policymakers and technologists must collaborate to ensure that innovation can thrive while also being subject to oversight and accountability. This is especially true when it comes to technologies that have the potential to impact society on a large scale, such as surveillance tools, AI, and big data systems.

Advocacy for Ethical Standards in Technology

Carl Pi's work has always been driven by a vision of technology that serves the greater good of society. However, he recognizes that without ethical standards to guide development, technological advancements can easily go astray. Throughout his career, Pi has advocated for the creation and implementation of ethical standards in the tech industry, pushing for a more responsible approach to innovation. Pi's advocacy for ethical standards is rooted in his belief that technology should enhance human life and promote societal well-being. This is particularly important in the realm of data analytics and surveillance, where the potential for harm such as privacy violations, discrimination, and unjust surveillance is high. Pi has called for the development of clear ethical guidelines that govern how data is collected, used, and protected, and he has emphasized the need for transparency and accountability in all aspects of technological development. One of the most significant ethical issues Pi has focused on is the importance of data privacy. In an era where personal information is constantly being collected and analyzed, Pi believes that individuals have the right to control their own data. He has advocated for laws that protect personal data and prevent companies from exploiting individuals' information for profit. However, he also recognizes that some level of data collection is necessary to address societal challenges, such as public health or national security. The key, he argues, is to find a balance between the benefits of data-driven innovation and the protection of individual rights.

Pi has also championed the need for fairness in the use of technology. AI and machine learning algorithms are powerful tools, but they are not without their biases. Pi has been a vocal advocate for the development of unbiased algorithms that are designed to treat all individuals fairly, regardless of race, gender, or socioeconomic status. He has called for greater transparency in how algorithms are designed and how decisions are made, urging companies to be accountable for the consequences of their technology.

Pi's advocacy for ethical standards extends beyond just his own company. He has been an active participant in discussions about the role of the tech industry in shaping policy and governance. By pushing for the development of clear ethical guidelines, Pi hopes to set an example for other tech leaders and policymakers, encouraging them to prioritize the responsible use of technology in their own work.

Carl Pi's Contributions to Policy and Governance

Carl Pi's influence in the tech world goes beyond his work at Palantir. He has also made significant contributions to policy and governance, advocating for laws and regulations that balance innovation with responsibility. As a leader in the tech industry, Pi has worked closely with policymakers, industry groups, and advocacy organizations to shape the future of technology and ensure that its benefits are distributed equitably.

One of Pi's most notable contributions to policy has been his work on data protection and privacy laws. In the wake of numerous data breaches and growing concerns about the misuse of personal information, Pi has been a strong proponent of stronger data protection regulations. He has argued that companies should be held accountable for how they handle personal data, and that individuals should have more control over their own information. This has led to his support of measures such as the General Data Protection Regulation (GDPR) in the European Union, which seeks to protect individuals' privacy and establish clear guidelines for data handling.

Pi has also been involved in discussions about the ethical implications of surveillance technologies, particularly in relation to national security. While he believes that surveillance can play a crucial role in protecting citizens from threats, he has called for stricter oversight and accountability in how surveillance data is collected and used. Pi has worked with lawmakers to ensure that privacy rights are respected and that surveillance technologies are deployed transparently and responsibly.

Beyond privacy and surveillance, Pi has also contributed to broader discussions about the regulation of AI and machine learning. As these technologies become increasingly integrated into everyday life, Pi has emphasized the need for ethical standards that govern their development and use. He has called for regulations that ensure AI is used to benefit society while preventing the perpetuation of biases or the concentration of power in the hands of a few tech giants.

Through his work with policymakers and advocacy groups, Pi has helped to shape the conversation around the intersection of innovation and governance. His contributions to policy and governance reflect his broader commitment to ensuring that technology is used responsibly and ethically. By engaging with regulators and industry leaders, Pi hopes to create a future where innovation and governance work hand in hand to foster a more equitable and sustainable society.

CHAPTER 6: THE LEGACY OF PALANTIR AND BEYOND

The story of Carl Pi is deeply intertwined with the rise and evolution of Palantir Technologies, the data analytics firm he co-founded. Palantir's legacy is one of both technological innovation and ethical controversy. Its role in revolutionizing the way data is used for intelligence and security purposes has been undeniable, but so too has the debate over the implications of such powerful tools. This chapter explores the legacy of Palantir, examining its influence on global intelligence and security, and considers what comes next for Pi as he moves beyond the company he helped build.

Building Palantir: A Data Analytics Revolution

Palantir Technologies was founded in 2003 with the goal of making data more accessible and usable for organizations, particularly in government and intelligence sectors. Carl Pi and his co-founders set out to create a tool that could analyze large and complex data sets to identify patterns and connections that might otherwise go unnoticed. The company's early focus was on using its software to combat terrorism and help intelligence agencies better track and understand terrorist networks. With Pi's vision, Palantir's data analytics platform quickly became indispensable for the U.S. government, particularly within agencies like the CIA, FBI, and NSA.

What set Palantir apart from other data analytics companies was its ability to work with disparate and unstructured data, such as surveillance footage, intelligence reports, and communications intercepts. Most traditional analytics platforms struggled to process this kind of unstructured data, but Palantir's software was built specifically to handle it, making it an invaluable tool for national security operations. This capability allowed intelligence agencies to use the data they already had in more effective ways, uncovering hidden threats and developing better strategies to prevent terrorist attacks.

Palantir's success in the intelligence community did not go unnoticed, and the company's influence quickly spread beyond government agencies.

Corporations, law enforcement agencies, and even non-profit organizations began to adopt Palantir's software to streamline their operations and improve decision-making. The company's ability to integrate vast amounts of data and produce actionable insights made it a powerful player in both the public and private sectors.

Palantir's rapid rise also attracted attention from critics, particularly regarding its role in surveillance and the ethical concerns surrounding the use of such powerful data analytics tools. The company's involvement in high-profile government surveillance programs, including those run by the U.S. military and law enforcement agencies, raised questions about privacy, civil liberties, and the potential for abuse of power. Despite this, Pi remained steadfast in his belief that Palantir's technology was being used for the greater good—to protect citizens and make the world safer. Palantir's legacy, therefore, is one of both innovation and controversy. The company transformed the way data is used in national security, corporate strategy, and law enforcement, but it also brought to the forefront important ethical questions about the balance between security and privacy. The legacy of Palantir is inextricably linked to the questions it raised about surveillance, governance, and the role of technology in society.

The Influence of Palantir on Global Intelligence and Security

Palantir's impact on global intelligence and security cannot be overstated. The company's software has been used in a variety of high-stakes operations, from tracking terrorist cells and preventing attacks to fighting drug trafficking and managing global health crises. Palantir's ability to process and analyze vast amounts of data from multiple sources has made it an invaluable tool for organizations that need to make sense of complex, fast-moving situations.

For example, during the operation to locate and eliminate Osama bin Laden, Palantir's software played a crucial role in analyzing data from a variety of sources intelligence reports, satellite imagery, and communications intercepts to build a clearer picture of bin Laden's whereabouts. The software allowed analysts to identify connections between different pieces of data that would have otherwise gone unnoticed, leading to the identification of the compound where bin Laden was hiding.

Palantir has also been involved in other critical areas, including disaster response and public health. During the Ebola outbreak in West Africa in 2014, Palantir's technology was used to track the spread of the virus and coordinate the response efforts. The company's ability to bring together disparate data sets and provide real-time insights proved essential in managing the crisis.

Palantir's influence on global intelligence and security is also reflected in its partnerships with governments and international organizations. The company has worked with intelligence agencies in countries around the world, including the U.K., Canada and Australia, helping to improve their ability to

analyze and act on intelligence. Its
global reach has solidified its position
as a key player in the field of data
analytics for national security and it
continues to shape the way
governments approach issues of
intelligence gathering, analysis, and
security.

Despite the praise for Palantir's role in
improving global security, the
company's involvement in
surveillance and data analysis has
raised concerns about the potential for
misuse. Critics argue that the
widespread use of Palantir's software
could lead to the overreach of
government surveillance, infringing on
the privacy rights of individuals. While
Pi has defended his company's work,
asserting that it is used to protect
society, the ethical questions
surrounding its role in surveillance
remain a central part of the
conversation about Palantir's legacy.

Carl Pi's Vision Post-Palantir: What's Next?

Although Carl Pi's work with Palantir
has cemented his place as a tech
innovator, his vision for the future

extends far beyond the company. As the founder and former CEO of Palantir, Pi has been instrumental in shaping the direction of the company and its impact on global security. However, he has always been focused on the broader implications of technology and its potential to improve society.

Looking ahead, Pi has expressed interest in exploring new areas of innovation, particularly those that intersect with social good and sustainability. His passion for creating technologies that can address global challenges, such as climate change, healthcare, and education, suggests that his future endeavors will be focused on using technology for the betterment of society. Pi's belief that technology can be a force for good continues to drive his work, and he has hinted at several new ventures that will focus on solving some of the world's most pressing issues.

While Pi's next steps remain to be fully seen, it is clear that he will continue to push the boundaries of what technology can achieve. His legacy at Palantir will undoubtedly continue to influence the tech industry, but his broader vision for the role of technology in addressing societal challenges will likely define his future work.

Palantir's impact on the world is undeniable, but its legacy is also a reminder of the complexities of innovation. Pi's work has changed the way we think about data, security, and surveillance, but it has also highlighted the ethical challenges that come with the power of technology. As Pi moves beyond Palantir, his continued focus on the responsible development of technology suggests that he will remain a key figure in shaping the future of tech, ensuring that innovation serves humanity's best interests.

CHAPTER 7: THE CONTROVERSIES AND CRITICISMS

Despite the immense success and technological breakthroughs that Carl Pi and Palantir have brought to the world, their work has not been without significant controversy. The company's role in national security, law enforcement, and surveillance has sparked an ongoing debate over privacy, civil liberties, and the ethical implications of big data. As powerful as Palantir's technology is, it has raised critical questions about the potential for misuse and the balance between national security and individual rights. This chapter explores the controversies surrounding Palantir and Carl Pi, examining public scrutiny, data privacy concerns, and the broader ethical dilemmas that come with technological advancements.

Facing Public Scrutiny and Ethical Dilemmas

One of the primary sources of controversy surrounding Palantir has been its close ties to government surveillance programs. Early on, Palantir's software was used to assist in intelligence gathering efforts, particularly by the U.S. government. While the company played a pivotal role in anti-terrorism operations and national security, this involvement also drew considerable public attention and criticism. Civil rights groups, privacy advocates, and even some politicians have raised concerns about the potential for Palantir's software to be used in ways that infringe upon civil liberties.

The most vocal criticisms center around the idea of "mass surveillance." Palantir's software enables agencies to collect, analyze, and correlate vast amounts of data from a variety of sources, including communications intercepts, financial transactions, and social media profiles. Critics argue that such capabilities, if unchecked, could lead to a level of surveillance that invades the privacy of ordinary citizens, potentially infringing on First Amendment rights and due process protections. They argue that Palantir's technology gives governments unprecedented access to individuals' private lives, with little oversight or transparency.

Carl Pi, while a staunch defender of his company, has often faced the brunt of these ethical concerns. He has had to publicly address accusations that

Palantir's work enables the government to overreach and violates privacy rights. Pi insists that Palantir's mission is to provide intelligence agencies with tools to protect society, arguing that national security must be balanced with privacy concerns. However, critics remain unconvinced, fearing that such powerful tools may be misused or that the line between necessary security measures and unjust surveillance could become increasingly blurred.

The ethical dilemma is not just about privacy, but about the potential for harm. With Palantir's powerful data analysis tools, the risk of mistakes and misinterpretations is high. What happens if faulty intelligence gathered through Palantir's software leads to an innocent person being wrongfully targeted or detained? What if biased data influences government decisions or law enforcement practices? These concerns are at the heart of ongoing debates about Palantir's role in government surveillance programs.

Data Privacy Concerns and the Palantir Debate

One of the most contentious issues surrounding Palantir is its handling of data privacy. As the company collects vast amounts of sensitive information, questions about how that data is stored, protected, and shared have surfaced time and time again. Data privacy is a cornerstone issue in today's digital age, and companies that handle personal information are under increasing scrutiny to ensure that their practices align with privacy laws and ethical guidelines.

Carl Pi has long maintained that Palantir takes data privacy seriously. The company's software, he argues, is designed to help organizations make sense of data without compromising individual privacy rights. However, critics argue that Palantir's very business model—collecting, analyzing, and storing vast amounts of data places it in a morally gray area. How can a company that builds its infrastructure around massive data collection ensure that it is not violating privacy rights? How does Palantir ensure that the data it uses for analysis does not contain personally identifiable information or violate privacy laws, especially in countries with strict privacy regulations like the European Union? While Palantir's software is capable of anonymizing data, many question whether this is enough to prevent privacy violations. The reality is that much of the data Palantir works with is not anonymized, and in some cases, it may contain highly sensitive information. Critics argue that even if data is anonymized, it can still be pieced together in ways that expose individuals' identities or behaviors. In a world where data can be used to predict behavior, make decisions, and even shape public opinion, the stakes are incredibly high. Data privacy concerns are not only about protecting individuals from identity theft or misuse of personal information, but also about protecting civil liberties and the right to freedom from unwarranted surveillance.

Pi has publicly responded to these concerns by arguing that Palantir's work is aimed at helping protect individuals by identifying and preventing threats before they materialize. For instance, Palantir's technology has been credited with helping thwart terrorist attacks and track criminal networks, tasks that arguably serve the public interest. However, the question remains: at what cost to personal privacy? The debate about Palantir's role in data collection, privacy, and surveillance has yet to reach a definitive resolution, with no clear answer to the ethical questions that continue to be raised.

Addressing the Challenges of Technological Overreach

A central theme in the criticisms of Palantir is the concern that technology, particularly when used by government agencies, can easily overreach its intended purpose. Palantir's ability to aggregate and analyze massive amounts of data allows it to uncover insights that would be impossible for traditional methods to detect. While this has clear benefits for national security, it also raises the question of where the line should be drawn. When does the use of technology to protect society cross the line into the realm of authoritarian control?

The fear of technological overreach is not limited to surveillance. In recent years, there has been growing concern over how technology, including AI and machine learning, is being used to make decisions about individuals' lives. Palantir's software is capable of providing insights that can influence critical decisions in areas such as law enforcement, criminal justice, and even employment. As Pi's technology becomes more widespread, the potential for misuse grows. What happens when algorithmic decisions made by AI systems are biased or flawed? How do we hold technology companies accountable when their software leads to harmful outcomes? Technological overreach also raises questions about the role of corporate influence in governance. Palantir's close relationships with government agencies, coupled with the immense power it wields through its data analytics tools, have led some to argue that the company has too much influence over the public sector. The concern is that such powerful tools could be used to push particular political agendas or make decisions that prioritize corporate interests over the needs of citizens.

Carl Pi has often defended Palantir's work by emphasizing that the company's mission is to help solve critical global challenges—protecting society from threats like terrorism, cyberattacks, and organized crime. However, the ethical implications of such a powerful tool being used in the hands of governments and corporations are complex. As technology continues to evolve, the challenge for Pi and other innovators in the tech space will be to ensure that their creations are used in ways that serve the greater good without infringing on the rights of individuals or the integrity of democratic systems.

CHAPTER 8: TECHNOLOGY, DEMOCRACY

AND THE FUTURE

As technology continues to shape our world, its influence on democracy and governance becomes an increasingly important issue. Carl Pi and his work at Palantir have been central to discussions about how technology impacts democracy both positively and negatively. Palantir's tools, which provide governments with powerful data analytics capabilities, have raised concerns about the balance between security and privacy, transparency, and the potential for authoritarian control. This chapter explores the complex relationship between technology and democracy, examining Carl Pi's views on the role of technology in democratic societies and how innovations can help or hinder democratic values.

The Role of Technology in Shaping Democratic Systems

In modern democratic systems, technology plays an essential role in governance, communication, and decision-making. Whether it is through social media platforms that enable public discourse or the use of data analytics to improve public policy, technology can empower individuals and institutions to act more efficiently and transparently. Carl Pi has long argued that technology, when used responsibly, can support democratic values by improving governance, promoting accountability, and increasing citizen participation.

For Pi, technology is not inherently good or bad it is how it is used that determines its impact on democracy. Palantir's software, for example, has been instrumental in helping governments and organizations identify threats, track criminal activities, and improve public services. In a world where information is power, providing governments with the ability to analyze and act on vast amounts of data can enhance decision-making processes, allowing for better-informed policies that respond to public needs. In this regard, technology can make democratic systems more efficient, transparent, and responsive.

He also acknowledges that the same technologies that can strengthen democracy can also be misused to undermine it. The very tools that Palantir develops to combat terrorism, crime, and other threats could be used to stifle dissent, track political opponents, or engage in mass surveillance. In this sense, technology poses a double-edged sword: it can either empower democratic institutions or erode them. Pi's stance on technology and democracy is rooted in the belief that safeguards must be in place to prevent abuse and ensure that innovation serves the public good, rather than consolidating power in the hands of a few.

As technology continues to advance, its role in shaping democratic systems will only grow more complex. Governments around the world are grappling with how to regulate new technologies while balancing innovation with the preservation of democratic values. Pi's work serves as a reminder of the critical importance of aligning technological development with ethical standards that protect the freedoms and rights of citizens.

Carl Pi's Views on Technology's Place in Society

Carl Pi's philosophy on technology is grounded in the belief that innovation should be used to solve pressing global challenges and enhance human well-being. From his early work with Palantir to his current focus on addressing issues like climate change and social inequality, Pi has consistently championed the idea that technology has the power to bring about positive change. However, his views on technology are tempered by a deep understanding of its potential dangers.

Pi argues that, while technology can drive progress, it must be developed and used with careful consideration of its societal impacts. As the founder of Palantir, he has witnessed firsthand the immense power that data analytics can wield. Yet, he is also aware of the risks that come with this power. In his view, it is not enough for technology to be innovative—it must also be ethical, transparent, and accountable. For Pi, the key to ensuring that technology serves the public interest is fostering a culture of responsibility within the tech industry.

In particular, Pi has been vocal about the need for ethical standards in data collection and analysis. He believes that, as data becomes an increasingly valuable resource, the potential for exploitation grows. Without robust ethical guidelines and regulations, technology companies could misuse data to manipulate public opinion, influence elections, or infringe on individual privacy. Pi's commitment to responsible innovation is evident in Palantir's approach to data—where he has emphasized transparency, privacy protections, and accountability. He believes that, with the right ethical framework in place, technology can be harnessed to serve the greater good without compromising individual rights.

While Pi's views on technology's role in society are rooted in optimism, they are also grounded in pragmatism. He recognizes that technology alone cannot solve the world's problems. It must be paired with thoughtful policy, collaboration between governments and private sector actors, and a commitment to fairness and justice. Technology, Pi argues, should complement human agency, not replace it.

Tech Innovations and Ethical Governance

As we look to the future, the intersection of technology and governance will become even more critical. Carl Pi's work has already highlighted how innovations in data analytics, artificial intelligence, and surveillance can transform the way governments operate. But with these advancements come significant challenges especially when it comes to ensuring that technology is used ethically and in a manner that respects democratic principles.

The next frontier in technology will likely involve further advancements in artificial intelligence, machine learning, and automation. These technologies have the potential to revolutionize industries from healthcare to transportation, but they also raise difficult questions about privacy, accountability, and the redistribution of power. Pi has repeatedly called for the development of ethical frameworks that can guide the responsible use of AI and other emerging technologies. These frameworks would need to address issues like data privacy, algorithmic bias, and the impact of automation on jobs and inequality.

Pi's vision for the future also includes a recognition of the need for more robust governance structures to oversee the development and deployment of new technologies. As technology continues to outpace regulatory frameworks, there is a growing concern that governments will be unable to keep up with the pace of innovation. Pi has emphasized the importance of collaboration between the tech industry, policymakers, and civil society to ensure that technology is developed in a way that aligns with democratic values.

In particular, Pi has called for greater transparency in the development of AI and machine learning systems. He believes that these technologies must be built with clear ethical guidelines that prioritize fairness and accountability. Moreover, he advocates for regulations that would require companies to disclose how their algorithms work and ensure that they are not being used to discriminate against certain groups of people. By fostering transparency and accountability, Pi hopes to prevent the potential misuse of technology and create a more equitable society.

As the world enters a new era of technological innovation, the ethical governance of these technologies will become increasingly vital. Carl Pi's work serves as a reminder that while technology can drive progress, it must be developed and deployed with caution and care. The challenges of balancing innovation with ethical considerations will shape the future of democracy, and it will be up to leaders like Pi and others in the tech industry to ensure that technology is used to support, rather than undermine, the values of democracy.

CHAPTER 9: THE ETHICAL CHALLENGES OF AN EVOLVING TECH LANDSCAPE

As technology continues to evolve at a rapid pace, the ethical challenges associated with it grow more complex and far-reaching. Carl Pi's work with Palantir has highlighted the potential benefits of advanced data analytics and artificial intelligence (AI) in solving global problems, but it has also brought to light the profound ethical dilemmas that accompany such innovations. In this chapter, we will explore the ethical challenges posed by new frontiers in AI, automation, and data collection, and discuss how innovators like Carl Pi are grappling with these challenges to ensure that technology is used for the benefit of society.

New Frontiers in AI and Automation

Artificial intelligence and automation are perhaps the most transformative technologies of the 21st century. AI's ability to process vast amounts of data, recognize patterns, and make predictions has already had a significant impact on industries ranging from healthcare to finance. In the future, AI has the potential to revolutionize nearly every aspect of society from autonomous vehicles to personalized medicine. However, these advancements also raise fundamental ethical questions.

One of the most pressing concerns is the potential for job displacement due to automation. Carl Pi has acknowledged that as AI and automation become more capable, they may render many traditional jobs obsolete. While this could lead to greater efficiency and economic growth in the long term, the immediate impact on workers particularly those in industries most susceptible to automation could be severe. The ethical challenge here lies in how to balance the benefits of technological progress with the social responsibility to protect workers and ensure a fair economic transition.

Pi has advocated for a proactive approach to addressing these concerns. He believes that society must anticipate the impact of AI and automation on the workforce and take steps to retrain workers, invest in education, and create new economic opportunities. Pi emphasizes the importance of creating social safety nets to support displaced workers during the transition to a more automated economy. By planning ahead and taking a holistic approach to the ethical implications of automation, society can mitigate some of the negative consequences while still reaping the benefits of technological progress.

Another ethical concern surrounding AI and automation is the issue of bias. AI systems, while powerful, are only as good as the data they are trained on. If that data is biased, the resulting AI models will also be biased. This has significant implications for decision-making in areas like criminal justice, hiring, and lending, where biased AI systems can perpetuate existing inequalities and discrimination. Pi has expressed concerns about the potential for AI to exacerbate societal divisions and reinforce systemic biases, particularly if companies are not transparent about how their algorithms work or if they fail to address biases in their data.

To address these issues, Pi has called for greater transparency and accountability in the development of AI systems. He advocates for the creation of ethical guidelines that require companies to disclose how their algorithms are trained, what data is used, and how biases are mitigated. He also supports the development of independent oversight bodies that can monitor AI systems and ensure they are being used fairly and responsibly. By creating more transparency and oversight, Pi believes that AI can be developed in a way that minimizes harm and maximizes benefit.

The Dangers of Unchecked Technological Power

One of the most significant ethical concerns surrounding the use of technology is the potential for unchecked technological power to undermine democratic values and human rights. As companies like Palantir continue to develop more powerful tools for data collection and analysis, the risk of these tools being misused by governments, corporations, or other powerful entities grows. Carl Pi has been acutely aware of this danger and has made efforts to ensure that Palantir's technology is used responsibly and ethically. However, the potential for abuse is always present when it comes to powerful technological tools.

The issue of unchecked technological power is particularly relevant when it comes to surveillance. Palantir's data analytics software has been used by governments around the world to monitor individuals and track activities, sometimes without sufficient oversight or accountability. While these technologies can be used to combat crime, terrorism, and other threats, they also have the potential to infringe upon individuals' privacy rights and civil liberties.

Pi has repeatedly emphasized the need for transparency and accountability when it comes to surveillance technologies. He believes that governments and companies must be open about how data is collected, how it is used, and who has access to it. Additionally, Pi advocates for robust regulatory frameworks that can ensure that these technologies are used in ways that protect privacy and uphold human rights. Without such safeguards, there is a real risk that surveillance technologies could be used for authoritarian purposes, stifling dissent, and undermining democratic freedoms.

Another aspect of unchecked technological power is the concentration of power in the hands of a few large tech companies. As companies like Palantir grow in size and influence, they have the potential to shape public policy, control the flow of information, and impact the lives of millions of people. Pi has expressed concerns about the growing power of big tech and the lack of accountability that often accompanies it. He believes that the concentration of power in the hands of a few companies can have detrimental effects on democracy, as these companies may prioritize profits over public welfare and use their influence to shape policy in ways that benefit their bottom line.

To address these concerns, Pi has advocated for stronger regulatory oversight of tech companies. He believes that governments must take a more active role in ensuring that large tech companies are held accountable for their actions and that their power is kept in check. This includes ensuring that companies cannot monopolize markets, manipulate information, or engage in practices that harm consumers or society at large.

Crafting a Framework for Future Tech Innovation

As the pace of technological innovation accelerates, it is crucial that society develops a framework to guide the ethical development and deployment of new technologies. Carl Pi has long believed that technology should be developed with the goal of improving society and addressing global challenges. However, he also recognizes that technological progress must be tempered by ethical considerations to ensure that innovation does not come at the expense of human dignity, privacy, or democracy.

Pi advocates for the creation of an ethical framework that can guide the development of emerging technologies like AI, blockchain, and data analytics. This framework should include principles of transparency, accountability, and fairness, and should be developed through collaboration between the tech industry, governments, and civil society. Pi believes that by establishing clear ethical guidelines, society can ensure that technology is developed in a way that benefits everyone, not just the powerful few.

Pi stresses the importance of global cooperation in shaping the future of technology. As technological advancements continue to have a global impact, it is essential that countries work together to develop international standards and regulations that can address the ethical challenges posed by new technologies. Pi's vision for the future of tech innovation is one where technology serves as a force for good helping to solve the world's most pressing problems while respecting the rights and freedoms of individuals.

CONCLUSION

As we come to the end of this exploration of Carl Pi's life, work, and philosophy, it's clear that his contributions to the tech world, particularly through Palantir, have left a profound mark on both the industry and the broader discussions surrounding the ethical implications of technological advancements. Pi's career represents a unique intersection of innovation, ethics, and the realization of technology's potential to address complex global challenges. In this conclusion, we will reflect on his legacy, the lessons learned from his work, and the ongoing challenge of balancing progress with responsibility.

Reflecting on Carl Pi's Impact on Technology and Ethics

Carl Pi's influence on technology is undeniable. His visionary leadership at Palantir revolutionized data analytics, turning vast amounts of raw information into actionable intelligence used by governments, corporations, and other organizations worldwide. Under his guidance, Palantir developed software that helped tackle global challenges, such as counterterrorism, fraud detection, and disaster response. In many ways, Pi's work paved the way for the modern data-driven world, where information and analytics shape decisions and policies on an unprecedented scale.

Yet, Pi's impact extends beyond the technical achievements of Palantir. As much as he is known for his innovations, he has also been an advocate for the ethical use of technology. Pi has consistently emphasized that innovation should not occur in a vacuum but must be balanced with a deep understanding of its societal consequences. His work has sparked vital conversations about the need for transparency, accountability, and ethical standards in technology development—particularly in areas like data privacy, surveillance, and artificial intelligence.

Through Palantir, Pi has also played a critical role in highlighting the ethical dilemmas that accompany powerful technological tools. While the software Palantir develops is used for critical purposes like fighting terrorism and tracking criminal activity, it has also drawn scrutiny for its potential misuse in mass surveillance and privacy violations. Pi's open engagement with these issues has made him a key figure in the ongoing debate over how to balance the benefits of technological innovation with the protection of fundamental human rights.

His legacy is one of both progress and caution. He has demonstrated that technology has the potential to solve some of humanity's most pressing issues, but he has also shown that, without careful consideration, it can perpetuate inequalities and violate civil liberties. His work serves as a reminder that, as we develop new technologies, we must remain vigilant

about their ethical implications and
ensure that they are used responsibly
for the greater good.

**Lessons for Future Innovators and
Policymakers**

Carl Pi's career offers valuable lessons
for both future innovators and
policymakers who are shaping the
future of technology. For innovators,
Pi's example underscores the
importance of balancing ambition with
responsibility. The pursuit of cutting-
edge technologies should not be solely
motivated by profit or the desire for
market dominance but should be
driven by a genuine desire to address
societal needs and improve lives. Pi's
commitment to ethical innovation
serves as a model for how technology
leaders can push the boundaries of
what's possible while remaining
grounded in ethical considerations.
Pi's work highlights the need for
technology companies to be
transparent and accountable in their
practices. As the tech industry
continues to grow in power and
influence, it is essential that companies
prioritize the public good, engage in

open dialogue with the public, and adhere to ethical standards that protect individuals' rights. Pi has shown that when companies take these steps, they can build trust with users and governments and contribute to the creation of a more just and equitable world.

For policymakers, Pi's career offers important lessons about the need for regulations that keep pace with technological advancements. As technology evolves, governments must take proactive steps to ensure that laws and policies protect citizens from potential harms while still fostering innovation. This includes creating frameworks for data privacy, establishing guidelines for the ethical use of AI, and ensuring that surveillance technologies are used in ways that respect fundamental rights. Pi's work illustrates the importance of collaboration between the tech industry, government, and civil society to create policies that are both effective and fair.

Another critical lesson from Pi's career is the need for global

cooperation in addressing the ethical
challenges of emerging technologies.
Many of the issues discussed in this
book, such as data privacy, algorithmic
bias, and surveillance, are global in
nature and cannot be solved by
individual countries acting alone. Pi
has long advocated for international
collaboration in shaping the future of
technology. By working together,
countries can develop standards and
regulations that ensure new
technologies are developed in ways
that benefit everyone, not just the
powerful few.

**The Ongoing Challenge of
Balancing Progress and
Responsibility**

Looking to the future, the challenge of
balancing technological progress with
ethical responsibility will only become
more pressing. As new technologies
continue to emerge such as AI,
quantum computing, and
biotechnology, the ethical dilemmas
associated with them will become even
more complex. These technologies
have the potential to revolutionize
industries, solve critical global

problems and improve lives, but they also pose significant risks if misused. The challenge for innovators, policymakers, and society at large is to ensure that progress does not come at the cost of human dignity, privacy or freedom. Carl Pi's work provides a blueprint for how to approach this challenge: by fostering a culture of responsibility within the tech industry, developing robust ethical frameworks for technology, and ensuring that technological advancements serve the public good. The lessons learned from Pi's career can guide future leaders as they navigate the ever-evolving landscape of technological innovation. Carl Pi's legacy is one of innovation, ethics, and a commitment to using technology for the greater good. As technology continues to shape our world, his work serves as a reminder that we must always consider the broader implications of our innovations. The challenge of balancing progress with responsibility is ongoing, but by following the example set by Pi and others, we can build a future where technology enhances human flourishing, protects our rights and strengthens democratic values.

www.ingramcontent.com/pod-product-compliance
Lightning Source LLC
LaVergne TN
LVHW051537050326
832903LV00033B/4287